THE CRUNCHY KID

LEARNS THE

COLORS

Written by: Angela Harders
Illustrated by: _______________

Copyright © 2021

Author and Illustrator: Angela Harders

All rights reserved. This book and any portion thereof may not be reproduced or used in any manner whatsoever without the express written permission of the author and/or illustrator except for the use of quotations in a book review.

Hello!
I'm Cam the Crunchy Kid!
Together, we will learn our colors!
But I need your help to add
some art to the pages.
Are you ready?
Let's go!

Red

What is red?

Raspberries

Apple

Roses

Can you draw a picture of your favorite thing that is red?

Orange

What is orange?

Carrots

Monarch
Butterfly

Orange
Juice

Can you draw a picture of your
favorite thing that is orange?

Yellow

What is yellow?

Lemon

Sunflower

Banana

Can you draw a picture of your
favorite thing that is yellow?

Green

What is green?

Cucumbers

Broccoli

Watermelon

Can you draw a picture of your favorite thing that is green?

Blue

What is **blue**?

Blueberries

Cornflower

Water

Can you draw a picture of your
favorite thing that is blue?

Purple

What is **purple?**

Eggplant

Cabbage

Lavender

Can you draw a picture of your
favorite thing that is purple?

Pink

What is **pink**?

Sweet Potatoes

Dragon Fruit

Echinacea

Can you draw a picture of your
favorite thing that is **pink**?

Brown

What is **brown?**

Almonds

Ginger

Honey

Black

What is black?

Black Beans

Sesame Seeds

Blackberries

Can you draw a picture of your favorite thing that is black?

What is white?

Coconut

Epsom Salt

Jasmine

Can you draw a picture of your
favorite thing that is white?

WHO IS A CRUNCHY KID?

"Crunchy" is a word that describes a person who strives to live a natural life. You may do all of these things - or perhaps just one or two, but a commitment to physical, mental, emotional, and spiritual health and wellness is the biggest sign that you're a crunchy kid in a crunchy family.

Crunchy Kids usually love to...

- breastfeed
- wear cloth diapers
- use amber necklaces
- take Epsom salt baths
- eat raw, organic foods
- go to the chiropractor
- avoid putting toxins in/on the body

- co-sleep with family
- do elimination communication
- use natural remedies
- be in a baby sling or carrier
- play outside barefoot
- homeschool
- and more!

For additional resources, please visit: www.peacefulworldschoolers.com.